Success With Numbers & Concepts

New York • Toronto • London • Auckland • Sydney
Mexico City • New Delhi • Hong Kong • Buenos Aires

Teaching *Resources*

State Standards Correlations

To find out how this book helps you meet your state's standards, log on to **www.scholastic.com/ssw**

Written by Danette Randolph
Cover design by Ka-Yeon Kim-Li
Interior illustrations by Sherry Neidigh
Interior design by Quack & Company

ISBN-13 978-0-545-20085-1
ISBN-10 0-545-20085-7

Introduction

Parents and teachers alike will find this book to be a valuable learning tool. Children will enjoy completing a wide variety of math activities that are both engaging and educational. The activities include mazes, hidden pictures, matching, and other fun ways to learn about basic math concepts. While engaged in these activities, children get practice in recognizing and counting numbers from 1 to 20. They will also learn about one-to-one correspondence, identify number words from one to twenty, and solve problems using pictures. Take a look at the Table of Contents and you will feel rewarded providing such a valuable resource for your children. Remember to praise children for their efforts and successes!

Table of Contents

Name _____

Circle and Square Search

Color each circle shape.

Color each square shape.

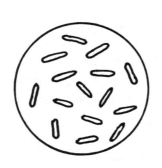

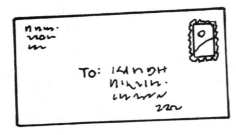

Name _____

Rectangle and Triangle Teasers

Color each rectangle shape.

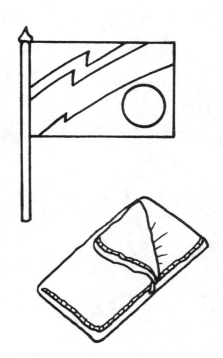

Color each triangle shape.

Oval and Diamond Detectives

Color each diamond shape.

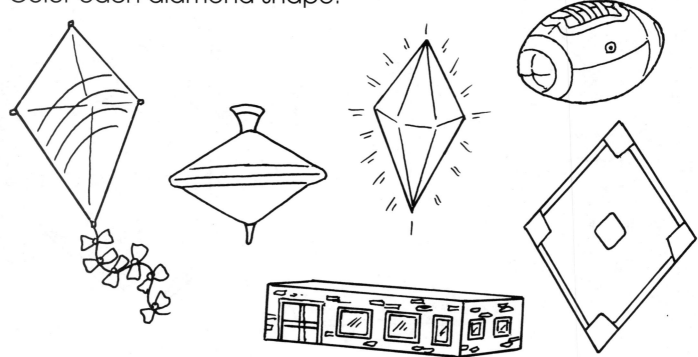

Color each oval shape.

Shape Matchup

Trace each shape. Draw a line to match each object to its shape. Color.

oval

rectangle

diamond

square

Zany Zoo Shapes

Color. ◇ = black   ☐ = blue   △ = red

 = brown   ◯ = green   ⬭ = yellow

Name _____

The Mole's Hole

Color each circle ◯ to show the mole's way home.

Name _____

Flying High With Shapes

Color. ◇ = purple ☐ = yellow △ = orange

▭ = green ◯ = blue ⬭ = red

1, 2 . . . Presents for You

Draw a circle around each group of 1.

Draw a square around each group of 2.

3, 4 . . . Let's Read More!

Draw a triangle around each group of 3.

Draw a diamond around each group of 4.

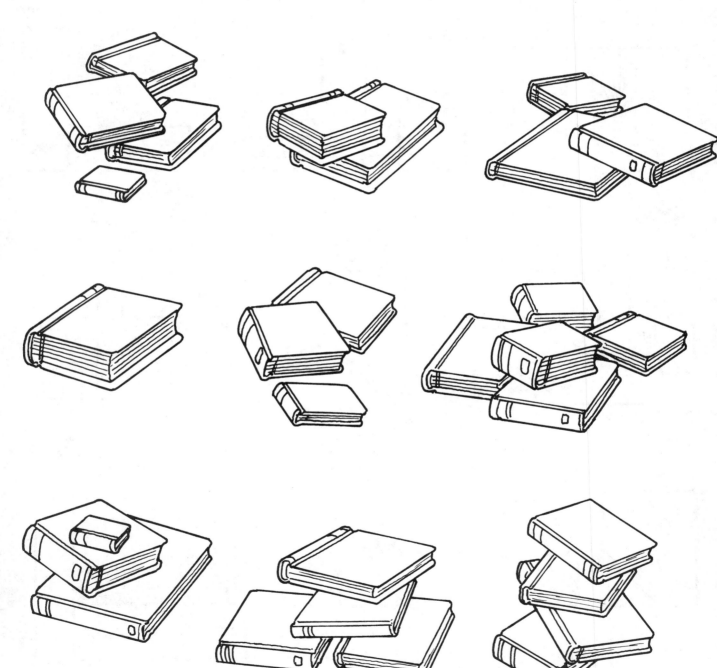

5, 6 . . . Flowers to Pick

Draw an oval around each group of 5.

Draw a rectangle around each group of 6.

7, 8 . . . Time to Skate

Color each group of 7 red.
Color each group of 8 yellow.

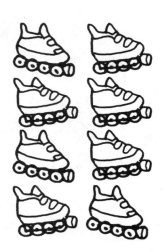

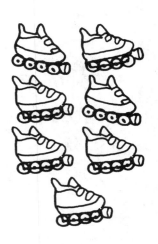

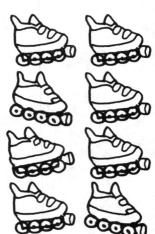

9, 10 . . . It's Fun to Win!

Color each group of 9 blue.
Color each group of 10 green.

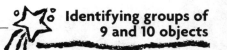

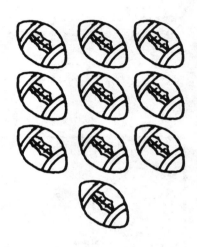

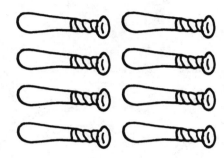

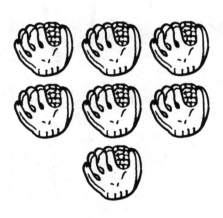

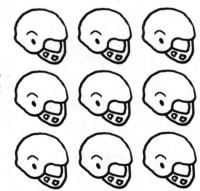

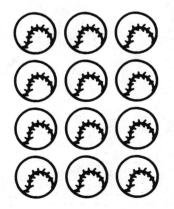

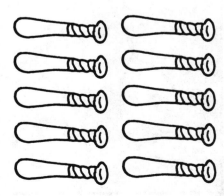

Bunny Number Fun

Color.

1 = pink	2 = green	3 = blue
4 = red	5 = brown	6 = yellow
7 = purple	8 = black	9 = orange

A Colorful Garden

•	yellow	:	pink	:	red
::	black	:.	orange	:::	purple
:.:	blue	:::::	green	:::	brown

Gumball Goodies

Color.

⠆	blue	⠦	red	⠒	green
⠿	orange	⠿	purple	⠿	black
⠿	brown	⠿	white	⠿⠿	yellow

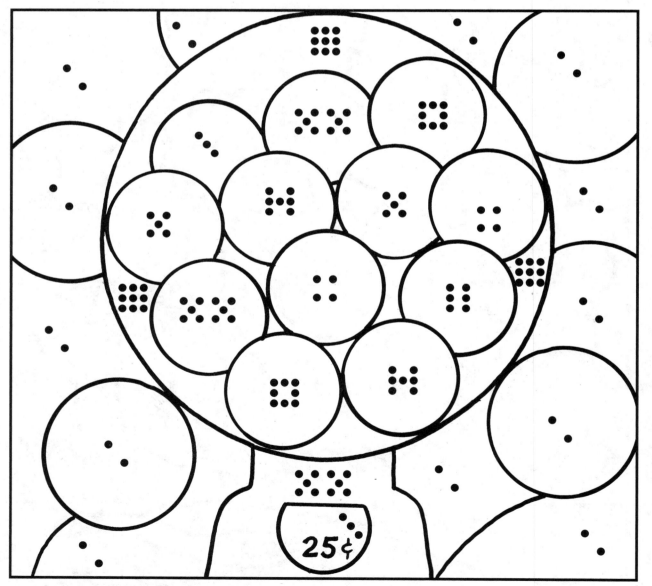

Name _____

Count and Color

Color the correct number of objects.

1	
6	
4	
10	
5	
2	
7	
8	
3	
9	

Lighten Things Up!

Connect the dots from **1** to **10**. Color.

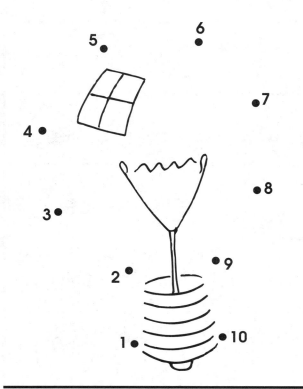

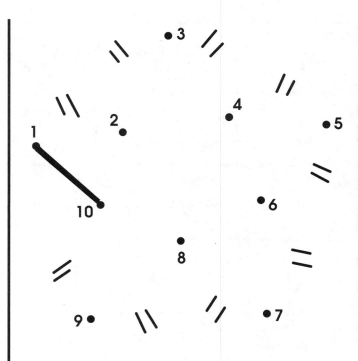

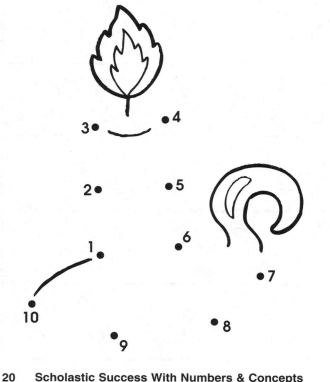

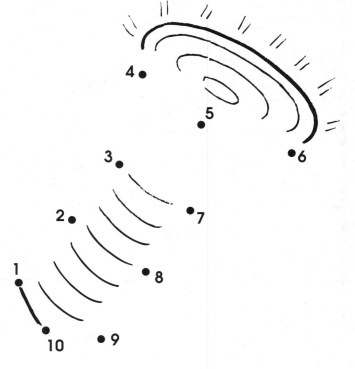

Calling All Alarms

Help the fire truck get to the fire. Color the path that goes in order from **1** to **10**.

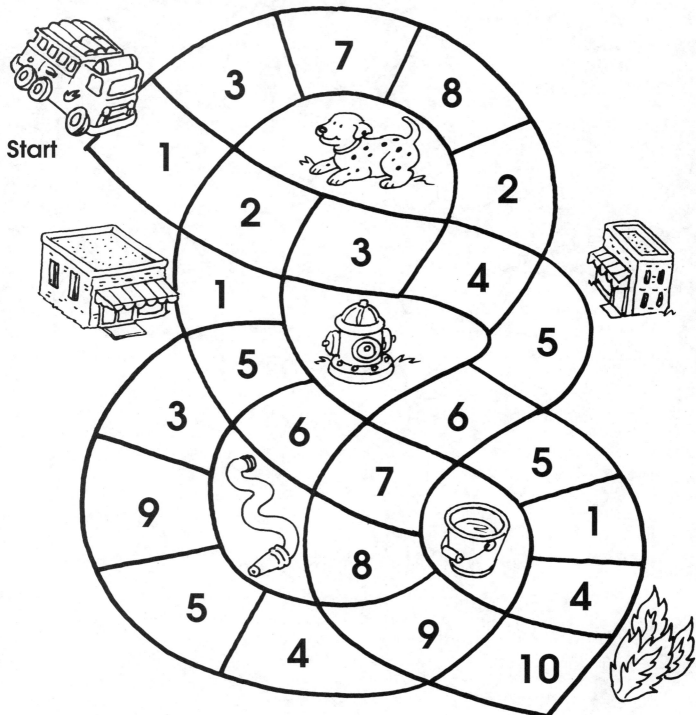

Home Sweet Home

Write each missing number.

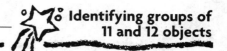

11, 12 . . . It's on the Shelf!

Draw a circle around each group of 11.

Draw a square around each group of 12.

13, 14 . . . Let's Play the Tambourine!

Draw an oval around each group of 13.

Draw a rectangle around each group of 14.

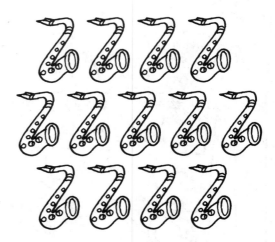

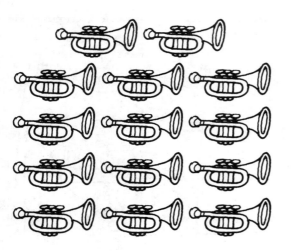

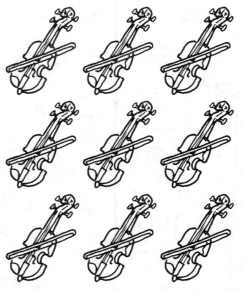

Name _____

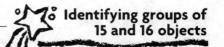

15, 16 . . . Eat Each Green Bean!

Draw a circle around each group of 15.

Draw a rectangle around each group of 16.

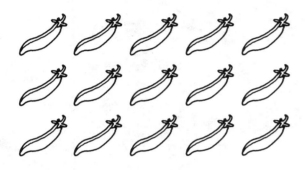

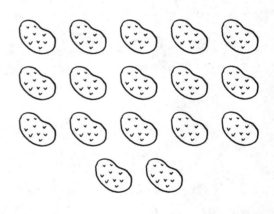

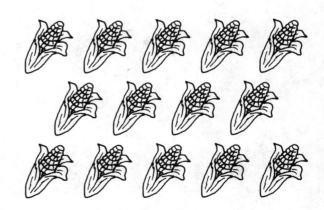

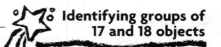

17, 18 . . . Don't Forget the Sunscreen!

Draw a circle around each group of 17.

Draw a square around each group of 18.

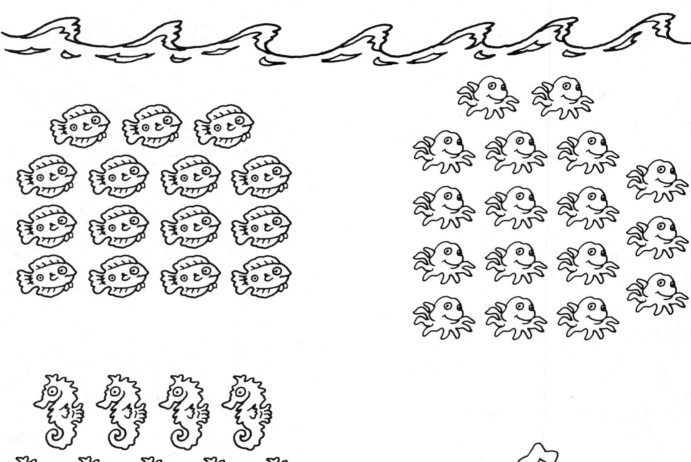

19, 20 . . . There Are Plenty!

Draw a circle around each group of 19.

Draw a square around each group of 20.

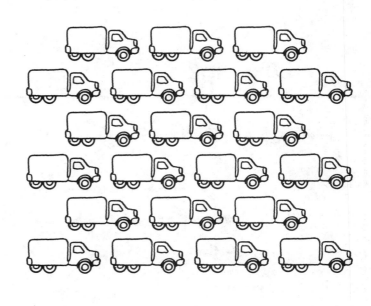

Time to Build

Color. 11 = yellow   12 = black   13 = blue

14 = white   15 = orange   16 = green

17 = red   18 = purple   19 = brown

20 = pink

Name _____

Let's Count!

Color the correct number of objects.

14	
12	
16	
11	
18	
15	
17	
13	

Fun Fruits

Match.

13

14

15

16

17

18

19

20

Name _____

Flying High

Color the bows on the tails to match the number above each kite.

Name _____

Juggling Act

Write each missing number.

Name _____

Each Number in Its Spot

Write each missing number.

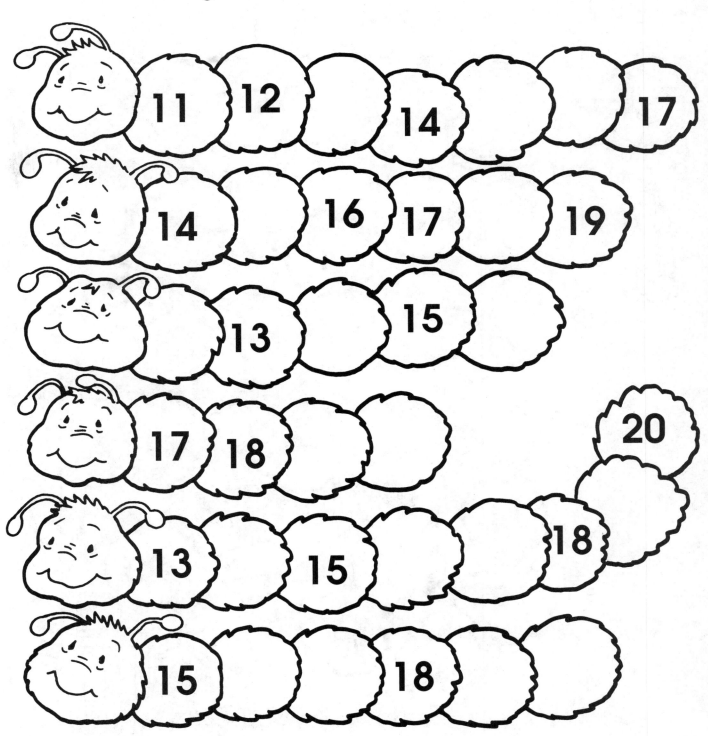

11 12 ☐ 14 ☐ ☐ 17

14 ☐ ☐ 16 17 ☐ 19

☐ 13 ☐ 15 ☐

17 18 ☐ ☐ 20 ☐ 18

13 ☐ 15 ☐ ☐ 18

15 ☐ ☐ 18 ☐

Name _____

Pick Up Trash!

Help the trash collector find his way to the trash can. Color
a path in order from **1** to **20**.

Keep On Trucking

Connect the dots from **1** to **20**.

Smiling Shapes

Draw a line to the shape that comes next.

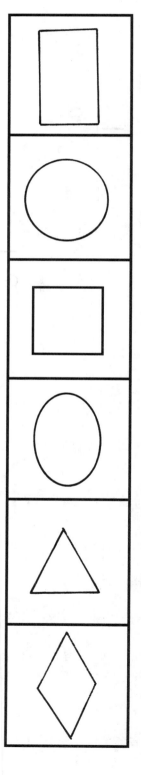

Ordering Outfits

Circle what comes next.

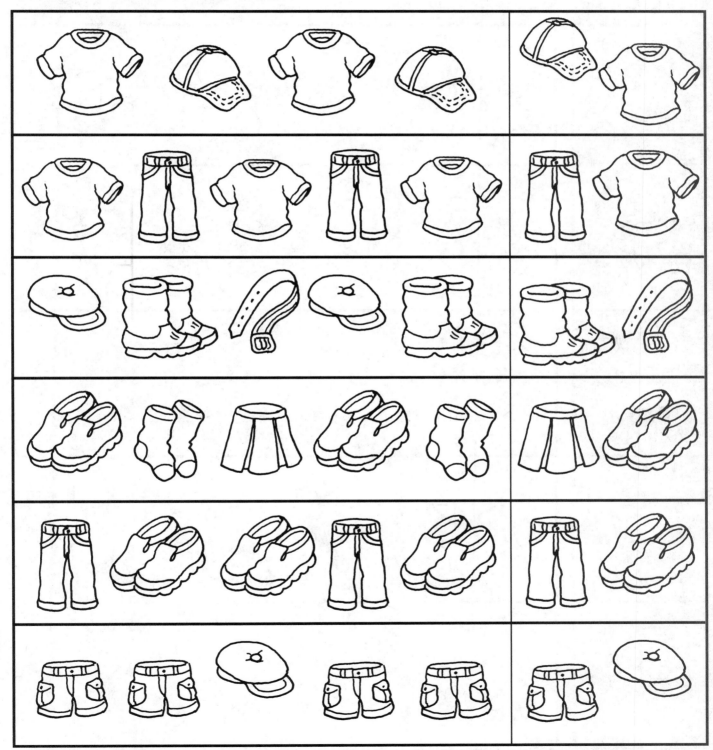

Look Alikes

Color the pictures with the same number as in the
first picture.

Just the Same

Match the groups with the same number.

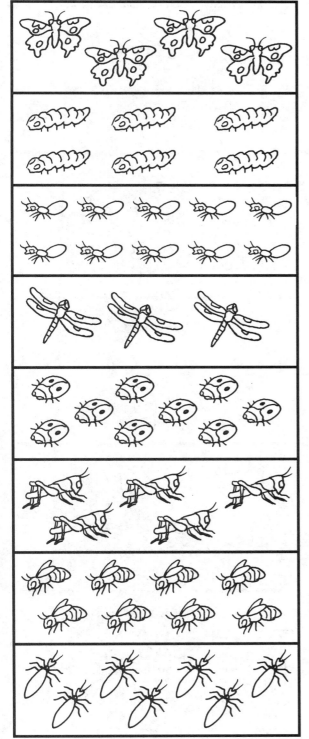
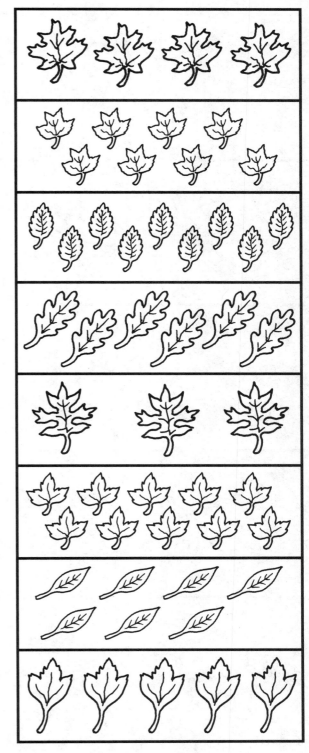

Name _____

Tasty Treats

Circle the one with more.

Name _____

A Little Snack

Circle the one with less.

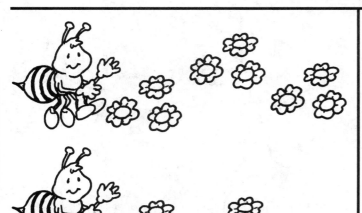

42

Name _____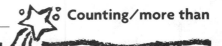

Sweet Spotted Buddies

Color the dog with more spots in each picture.

Name _____

Moving Along

Look at the picture.

Write the number.

How many?

| ☐ ✈ | ☐ 🚚 | ☐ 🚐 |
| ☐ 🚗 | ☐ 🚁 | ☐ 🚲 |

How many in all?

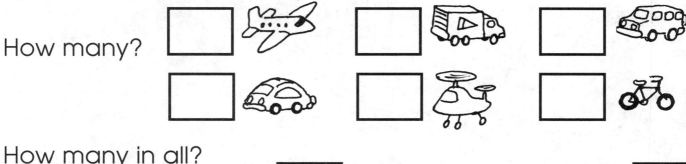

✈ and 🚗 ☐   🚚 and ✈ ☐

🚐 and 🚲 ☐   🚐 and 🚁 ☐

🚗 and 🚚 ☐   🚁 and ✈ ☐

A Perfect Day at the Park

Circle how many you see in the picture.

🚲	1	5
🪑	4	2
🌻	8	5
🛝	6	3
🌳	7	10
🐕	2	8
🐦	9	7
🐿️	10	7
🛴	3	1

Circle how many you see in all.

🐦	+	🚲	=	8 9 10
🌻	+	🛝	=	3 8 9
🪑	+	🐕	=	6 2 4

Teeny Tiny Garden Friends

Look at the picture.

Write the number.

How many?

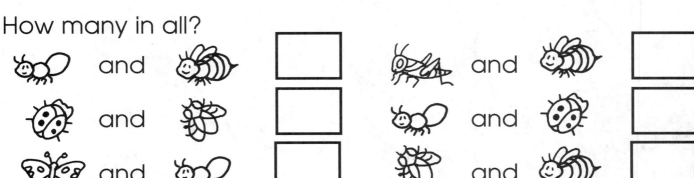

How many in all?

Name _____

Easy as One, Two, Three

Color.

one = yellow   two = black   three = blue

four = white   five = orange   six = green

seven = red   eight = purple   nine = brown

ten = pink

Name _____

Busy Bees

Count the bees in each picture.

Circle the correct number word.

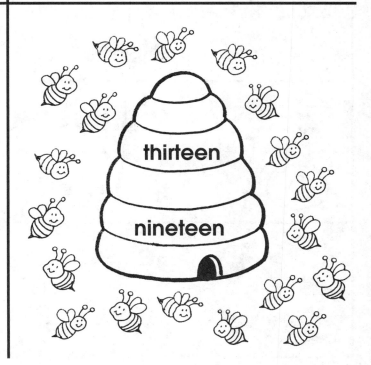

Name _____

Lovely, Little Ladybugs

Count the spots on each picture.

Circle the correct number word.

	one **five**		**two** **seven**
	fourteen **sixteen**		**nineteen** **fifteen**
	ten **eleven**		**twenty** **twelve**
	eighteen **thirteen**		**nine** **eight**
	seven **four**		**seven** **three**